We Did It,
Now Get Off Your Hindparts!
You Can Too

Dr. Yvette Harris
Blaque Diamond
LaSonja Brooks
Fairren McLemore
Dr. Briget Lovelace
LaToshia Simpson
Michelle Boulden-Hammond
Dr. Sharnice Perryman
Chelsia McCoy
Dr. Deborah Franklin
Dr. Keba Richmond Green
Syreeta Duncan

ISBN # 979-8-9926537-1-7

Printed in the United States of America.

Publisher: DF Publishing (https://deborahfranklinpublishing.com/about)

Book Cover Design: Brandon Jolly

Editor, Page Format/Layout: Chelsia McCoy/*Your Writing Table* (www.yourwritingtable.com)

Table of Contents

I declare and decree that
when I look in the mirror,
I will only see greatness
and the queen that I was
created to be.
My crown may get tilted
but it will never fall off.
I am positioning myself
to be in the winner's circle.
~Deborah Franklin

Introduction

We Did It, Now Get Off Your Hindparts! You Can Too is a collaboration of stories from women who have triumphed in the face of adversity to remind you that you can take charge of your life and move forward. You don't have to stay in the place you are. You don't have to be weighted down by despair, sorrow or shame. You can lift your head high and move to the next level to reclaim your greatness.

So many times in life we have been burdened down in the darkness of our minds to believe that we are the only one going through a particular situation. Trust me, I have been there. I let my mind take over and was lost in a dark place. I was wounded by past relationships and the loss of something I prayed for. Yes, I was in a place of no return, or at least that was how I was feeling. I was not in control of my feelings.

My solution was simple: I had to get off my 'hind parts' and make something happen. Getting off your hind parts is something as simple as changing the colors that you're wearing or looking for a different direction to take to work. No, don't get me wrong, it's not easy, but you have to do something.

As I was going through my darkest place and feeling like I had hit rock bottom, I was walking and talking in a daze, but I knew I had to do something. I had to reconnect with the world and make a conscious decision to take hold of the adage: *the biggest sign of insanity is to continue to do the same thing over and over again and expecting different results.* I knew I had to get off my hindparts and make something happen.

I got off my hindparts and started to join meetings with people that didn't want to take from me, but would pour their knowledge into me. I got off my hind parts and made connections with people I wasn't even sure could assist in moving the needle forward into the direction to change my current state of mind. I got off my hind parts, sought after coaches and training to increase my knowledge. But one of the biggest things I got off my hind parts and started to believe in myself. Changing my mindset was the biggest lift that I needed to reach higher heights.

You have made the biggest step by picking up this book to join the journey with the other women who have experienced major setbacks but made the hard conscious decision to get off their hind parts and make it happen, and you can, too.

Inherited Dreams:
Breaking Through Fear & Limitations
Dr. Yvette Harris

My mother was a symphony of resilience. A full-time working woman who was an African American executive Administrative Assistant (secretary in the 1970's) for a major oil company who simultaneously ran her own clothing design business (side hustle), she embodied entrepreneurship long before I understood what that word meant. Even battling a chronic autoimmune disease for a decade, she never stopped creating, never stopped dreaming. As a teenager, her entrepreneurial spirit flowed through me. Together, we would canvas our neighborhood, marketing my babysitting services.

By the age of 14, I had two younger clients that I babysat for Monday through Friday, along with other children, who came to my home during the weekends. At 14 years old, I was making a steady $50 a week and even more money on the weekends. Those early days taught me the fundamentals of business: networking, service delivery, and building trust within a community. Yet, despite witnessing my mother's tenacity, fear became my closest companion. I was convinced I wouldn't live past 48 – the age my mother passed away. This belief became a psychological prison, preventing me from fully embracing my entrepreneurial potential.

My educational journey mirrored this internal struggle. The only consistent "A" I received in grade school was in gym class. I began college at 17, only to drop out four times before finally committing to my academic path at 28. While only ending my bachelor's degree with a 2.49 GPA, persistence became my silent rebellion against self-doubt. When I finally completed my doctorate at 50, it wasn't just an academic achievement – it was a declaration of my own capabilities. While completing my education, I would begin what would become a wonderful career as an educator and catalyst for my business. During those 21 years, I would go from an entry level employee to a teacher, a counselor, principal and site and district level administrator.

At the age of 52, I jumped into full-time entrepreneurship. EDR Consulting and Training wasn't just a business; it was my declaration of independence from fear. My company is named after my mother, Elaine Deloras Randolph. Each year since starting, my income and vision have grown exponentially, proving that potential has no expiration date.

My journey teaches a profound lesson: entrepreneurship isn't about perfect timing or fearlessness. It's about forward movement, despite uncertainty. My mother's legacy wasn't just her business or her resilience – it was her unspoken message that limitations are often self-imposed. To every woman reading this: Your dreams don't have an age limit. Your potential isn't defined by past setbacks or internalized fears. Whether you start at 22 or 52, your entrepreneurial journey is valid, powerful, and uniquely yours.

My mother might not have lived to see my success, but her spirit dances with every client I serve, every training I deliver, and every barrier I help others overcome. Entrepreneurship isn't just a career – it's a courageous conversation with yourself about what's possible.

Dr. Yvette Monique Harris:
A Transformative Educational Leader and Entrepreneur

Dr. Yvette Monique Harris is a dynamic educator, entrepreneur, and proud United States Air Force veteran who has dedicated her professional life to empowering marginalized and underrepresented populations. As founder and CEO of Education and Development Resources Consulting and Training, Inc. (EDR), she leverages over 30 years of educational experience to provide high-impact training and coaching to veterans.

With a Doctorate in Education Leadership and two master's degrees, Dr. Harris has served in diverse roles including teacher, counselor, principal, and administrator. Her career has been defined by a passionate commitment to narrowing achievement gaps and creating transformative learning experiences for youth and adults.

As a Certified John Maxwell Trainer, Speaker, and Coach, Dr. Harris specializes in developing specialized training programs in entrepreneurship, workforce development, and leadership. Her client portfolio includes former professional athletes, re-entry populations, and emerging entrepreneurs. Dr. Harris's signature philosophy, "Don't try, be and do, so that you may have," encapsulates her belief in active personal transformation. Through EDR, she continues to create inclusive learning environments that inspire individuals to unlock their full potential and achieve unprecedented personal and professional success.

No mask that is hiding

me from my success will

be removed and will not

hold me back. From this

day forward, I will no

longer operate as a counterfeit

but in true authenticity.

~Deborah Franklin

NOTES

_____

_____

_____

_____

_____

_____

_____

_____

_____

_____

_____

_____

_____

NOTES

Accused, Investigated, and Vindicated: A Truth the System Can't Keep Ignoring

Blaque Diamond

Are they kidding me? Me, of all people?

I was the one who parented twelve children. Now, I am wrongfully accused of child abuse. These accusations are among the most challenging and devastating experiences of my life. As a caregiver and social worker, I dedicated my life to advocating for the well-being of children, especially those with special needs. I thought I could rely on the system that I worked with to provide resources, support, and services for my adopted child, who was eventually diagnosed with severe mental health challenges. However, instead of receiving the help I needed, I was under intense scrutiny, facing untrue allegations damaging my reputation, career, and family.

Accusations stemmed from my child's state of mind; the behaviors became increasingly difficult. In a moment of distress, my child made accusations that triggered an investigation, and suddenly, I was on the other side of the system. Despite over forty years of experience and my history of advocating for vulnerable children and adults, I was dealt with as if I were guilty before there was any confirmation of the allegations.

The investigative process was emotionally exhausting and professionally humiliating. The system questioned my character, my parenting was scrutinized, and my career was placed in jeopardy. I had to fight to keep my name and integrity intact and for the ability to continue doing the work I am passionate about it.

Eventually, my child admitted the truth that the accusations were false and a manifestation of her mental health. Although they overturned the charges, the damage lingered. My record, though cleared, will still bear the weight of suspicion in the eyes of many who will believe I am guilty, which is far from the truth. These accusations led me to step away from the direct child welfare field.

Rather than allow this injustice to define me, I turned my pain into purpose. I transitioned my role in social work to training future social workers on policy and practice to emphasize the (FACTS) Fair, Accurate, Concise, and Truth I am working to ensure that social workers understand the profound impact of their decisions on children and families caught in the process.

I cannot tell you the importance of thoroughly investigating allegations, avoiding biases, and treating families with dignity and respect while ensuring the best interest of the child's safety. My experience is not to garner sympathy but to have a just system for the field of social work and ensure future social workers are working with wisdom, integrity, and compassion.

I will uphold the Social Work Code of Ethics with continued advocacy for children and families in a manner that garners protection and justice. Turning adversity into action has renewed my purpose and allowed me to commit to preserving the integrity of the field of social work.

Blaque Diamond, also known as the **Perfectly Imperfect Parent**, is a **Social Worker, International Speaker, Parent Life Coach, and award-winning author** dedicated to empowering families and advocating for foster care, adoption, and reunification. She holds both a **BSW and MSW from Morgan State University** and has parented **twelve children**, including biological, adopted, and foster children.

Her literary works, including *She Named Me Stacey* and *The Habitchual Liar*, have gained **critical acclaim**, showcasing her ability to address complex themes with authenticity. As the host of *Basic Blaque After Dark*, airing on the **first and third Friday of each month at 8 PM EST**, she creates a platform for **diverse guests**, from authors to mental health advocates, engaging in meaningful conversations that resonate with her audience.

Next season, Blaque Diamond expands her platform with *Cracks in the Surface, Strength in the Core: Not Easily Broken*, a panel dedicated to **resilience and healing**. Her unwavering commitment to advocacy has earned her prestigious recognition, including the **Langston Hughes Excellence in Literature Award**, the **Indie Author Legacy Awards Community Champion Legendary Honoree**, and the **Beyond the Abuse Lifetime Achievement Award**.

Through her work, Blaque Diamond continues to inspire, educate, and advocate, ensuring that every child and family receives the support and understanding they deserve.

My strength empowers me to pursue my dreams relentlessly and I am grateful for the abundance that surrounds me.

~Deborah Franklin

NOTES

_____

_____

_____

_____

_____

_____

_____

_____

_____

_____

_____

_____

NOTES

How To Recover After Losing Your Mother & Best Friend

LaSonja Brooks

January 23, 2017, a day like no other. A day filled with life and wonderful expectations. As the day began, I was sitting nervously in the doctor's office with my mother, talking about going to Walmart, when the doctor enters. A quick greeting, then it was down to business.

The words that proceeded out of his mouth put us both on another trajectory. "I'm so sorry, but you have seven weeks."

My sharp response was, "Seven weeks for what?"

My mom, seated to my left, gives a half-hearted smile, and nodded, as if she knew. I literally turned my face to the wall, fighting back the tears as he continued to speak.

Mom had HR+HER2 Breast Cancer. Once I was able to gather my countenance and cleared my throat, I responded, "You do know today is her birthday."

He quickly looks at her chart and apologizes profusely.

Mom, being the sweet loving person that she was, and responds, "It's alright."

The doctor was correct. Approximately seven weeks later Monday, March 20, 2017, my mom, my best friend transitioned.

Standing bed side, breathless, as tears stream down my face, there I stood clinching her cold hand.

These past several years have been surreal and extremely challenging. I had to fight with everything within me because my number one fan and cheerleader was gone. How do you do life without the one that introduced you to the world? It was painfully difficult but I had to honor her and what she stood for, and what she stood on: the Word of God and the love of Jesus. If I was to survive, I had to get and stay focused. I had to make a conscious effort to commit to staying sane. I not only lost my mother, but my best friend.

On this journey to recovery, I was able to hold on to the many real-life conversations my mother and I shared. It is those real tough life conversations, and encouragement that has truly kept me. Every time I found myself wandered into the cave of loss; I was able to lock-hold to a shared encouraging moment. Another resource I tapped into is called TIME. There is an adage that says, "*time heals all wounds.*" This was key for me because I did not allow the opinions of others to dictate and peg my timeline to grieve. I allowed myself the necessary time to grieve, and to grieve as healthy as possible. I grieved at my own pace and in my own space.

Of course, I will never forget the fun-loving memories of her smile, touch, and warm hugs, and she always smelled so good. With every birthday, holiday, Mother's Day, meaningful events, ministry assignment, and road trip, I am joyfully reminded that my cheerleader is still cheering me on, it is just from another location. For me, giving up, is never an option.

LaSonja Brooks, aka "LaLa," is known for her charismatic personality and transparent lifestyle. She has shared the love of God through word and song for many years. She is the Executive Director and Founder of Another Chance Enrichment Center, the Founder and Visionary of The LG Effect Ministries, and Weddings and Events by LaSonja, LLC.

LaSonja currently serves as a worship pastor, motivational inspirational speaker, entrepreneur, author, reconstruction strategist, worship coach, podcaster, content creator, actress, and a proud mother and grandmother, affectionately known as G-LaLa.

LaSonja, is a graduate of Grand Canyon University, Phoenix, AZ, and The Logos Institute School of the Prophetic, Baton Rouge, LA.

LaSonja's favorite scripture, **Jeremiah 29:11:** *"For I know the thoughts that I think toward you, saith the Lord, thoughts of peace, and not of evil, to give you and expected end."*

I declare and decree that this is my season to activate. All that God has shown me will come forth. I know that my faith will be tested, but I won't be discouraged. I will stand strong.

~Deborah Franklin

NOTES

NOTES

The Beauty in the Unexpected
Fairren McLemore

Parenting is a journey full of love, hope, and challenges, but raising a child with a disability or special needs brings unique complexities that can test the strongest of hearts. For many parents, the initial diagnosis feels like stepping into a whirlwind of emotions, fear, uncertainty, guilt, and grief. It is a journey that often begins in darkness, but with time, resilience, and love, it becomes a path filled with light and growth.

When my daughter was diagnosed with Incontinentia Pigmenti, I found myself facing emotions I never thought I would experience as a parent. I questioned my own abilities, blamed myself for circumstances beyond my control, and mourned the life I imagined for her. Sleepless nights were consumed with "what if" scenarios, and the pressure to be strong felt overwhelming.

I also struggled with societal perceptions. The stares, the unsolicited advice, and the pity in people's eyes often weighed heavier than the diagnosis itself. I feared that her uniqueness would limit her opportunities or prevent her from experiencing the world fully. These dark thoughts were isolating, but they were also a turning point.

The breakthrough came when I realized I did not have to

do this alone. Seeking God and support, whether from friends, family, or professionals was not a sign of weakness but a step toward strength. I found community in other parents who were navigating similar paths. Their shared stories were a source of comfort and a reminder that I was not alone. When I began to see my daughter not through the lens of her diagnosis but as the radiant, strong, and vibrant person she is, it was a pivotal moment that changed my perspective. It was not about fixing her or the situation; it was about embracing her for who she is and celebrating her journey.

I embraced the process, educated myself, and built a support system. I celebrate milestones, practice self-compassion, and focus on advocacy and awareness. The path of raising a child with special needs is not linear, and there will always be moments of doubt, but through each challenge, I have learned to embrace the unexpected beauty of this journey. My daughter has taught me resilience, unconditional love, and the importance of seeing strength in differences.

What once seemed like a road paved with uncertainty has become a pathway of hope, purpose, and boundless joy. By focusing on solutions and leaning on love, I have learned that even the darkest moments can give way to the brightest light. And in that light, my daughter shines, and so do I.

Fairren McLemore, a native of Saint Joseph, Michigan, and raised in Elkhart, Indiana, is a passionate author and leader with a master's degree in organizational leadership. Her faith in God keeps her anchored and gives her the strength to keep moving forward in life. From a young age, she felt a deep calling to inspire and uplift others. Her mission is to be a source of light and hope in a world that can sometimes feel overwhelming. She firmly believes that you cannot pour from an empty cup, so she prioritizes self-care to pour into the lives of others.

Her debut book, *Shining Through: My Journey with Incontinentia Pigmenti*, was inspired by her daughter to turn personal experience into a book. Watching her navigate life with strength and resilience made Fairren realize how powerful sharing their story could be. She wanted to help others embrace differences, find beauty in challenges, and learn self-love. Writing this book became her way of giving a voice to their experiences, hoping to encourage other families facing their own unique battles. Currently residing in Fort Wayne, Indiana, Fairren enjoys spending time with her husband and two children who inspire her every day.

NOTES

NOTES

Finding the True Worshipper, the True Believer in Me
Dr. Briget Lovelace

Joy bleeding out of my heart, loneliness invading my spirit, and numbness crying out of my soul were piercing emotions that flooded me eleven years ago after three failed marriages. Hurts, pains, disappointments all keep pulling at my skirt tail trying to get me to look back with anguish to press the heart of God to take vengeance on my behalf. I had strived to find "that" relationship which would bring complete wholeness; everything of which a person might dream.

What I found instead is not what I dreamed of. It was extramarital affairs that broke my heart. Have any of you experienced pain like this? I trusted in relationships that ultimately failed.

As a reader of this chapter, one might wonder what the above paragraph has to do with the chapter's title. Believe me, there is a connection. Years ago, the Holy Spirit was trying to show me something. During that season, I served as a minister and leader in my local church. I poured myself into serving whenever leadership called. However, like so many other Christians, I experienced disappointment in God's house because some leaders chose to break covenant with God and man. This did not influence my service, but serving was not enough. Something was still missing. The Holy Spirit was gently nudging me trying to get my attention while I was spending solo time in my quiet place at dawn with God in prayer.

Fierce were the smiles I carried on my face masking the riveting thoughts that kept flooding my mind of having "that" relationship, which would complete me and escape my time here on earth. So, I looked forward to those brilliant gates laced with pearls, sparkling streets paved with gold, and my illuminated mansion in heaven. I put my flit towards seeking God's face.

While on my knees, the Holy Spirit changed my heart and healed my pain. He led me to 1 Peter 2: 1-5 to put aside all of the malice I carried from bad relationships, to forgive all those who had intentionally devise schemes to destroy me, and to allow Him to share the love of God through me. The more I sought out God's face the more peace I found. Joy took a hold of my spirit and soul like an ice skater's death spiral.

It was the pain and hardships I had experienced in past relationships that led me to the heart of true worship. I found the relationship I was looking for that I had had all the time - a relationship with Christ Jesus. In that revelation, I found the true worshipper and the true believer in me.

Dr. Briget Mirandra Lovelace - playwright, director, actress, prophetess, minister, teacher, and woman of God - was born in LaGrange, Georgia to Mr. and Mrs. Jimmy and Mary Lovelace, Sr. She was raised in Atlanta, Georgia where in her former years she attended Walter Frances White Elementary, Gresham Park Elementary, and Walker High School.

During her early childhood years, God gave her a love and desire to pursue His Word and theater. She attended Georgia State University and earned a bachelor's degree in communication with a concentration in theater and a minor in education. This was a springboard which led her to create Lovelace Theater Production Company to write, produce, and direct over 12 plays that illustrate how the power of prayer can change things.

Continuing her education, she earned a master's degree in secondary education language arts, a master's degree in leadership, an educational specialist degree in curriculum and instruction, and a doctoral degree in theology. In Gadsden, Alabama, she served in ministerial leadership under Apostle Melvin Crook and Pastor Willie Joe Simmons at New Liberty Tabernacle of Praise, and Pastor Reginald Huff at Bride of Christ. During her time in Gadsden, Dr. Lovelace worked in the Gadsden City Schools System as an English teacher, drama teacher and coach, assistant principal, and the Education Community Liaison.

After almost 27 years of service, she retired to return back to Georgia to the classroom in the DeKalb County School System currently serving as the Chairperson of the ELA Department and drama teacher and coach at Dr. Ronald E. McNair High School. Dr. Briget

Lovelace plans to produce more plays that will encourage, educate, and inspire others to be the best they can be while seeking God in prayer.

My name will be great in the presences of all men and women. I will operate in excellence and pure authenticity. All of my products and services will be sought after near and far.

~Deborah Franklin

NOTES

NOTES

Incarcerated

LaToshia Simpson

It all started in December 1994. I worked in the credit department of a high-end store for about a year. My job involved handling customer calls about their credit card accounts. Around that time, I had friends who often talked about scamming people. I dismissed their conversations with a "get a job" attitude, thinking I was immune to their influence. However, their words had unknowingly planted a seed in my subconscious. The Bible warns in 1 Corinthians 15:33: "Do not be deceived: Evil company corrupts good habits." Over time, their influence affected my mindset, leading me to make regrettable choices.

One day, while working at my desk, a thought crossed my mind: What if I tried it? A gentleman called to close his account, but instead of moving on, I reopened it. I shared his details with a friend, and together we devised a plan. We used his information to make purchases, exploiting the system without considering the consequences. At the time, the rush felt exhilarating, but I was on a dangerous path.

Everything came crashing down. Human Resources called me in, followed by the loss prevention officer and eventually the police. I faced a felony charge and probation. Did I mention I had a 3-year-old son? I was given probation and unfortunately, I violated it and served six months in state prison and yes, I saw a lot and experienced a lot during that time. The experience was life changing. There were many insulting moments.

From the time you walk in the door you are watched. The most humiliating thing is stripping out of all your clothes in front of people you don't know. The way they talk to you is degrading. I learned really quick this was a place I didn't want to return to. I had to do two weeks in solitary confinement for finding an officer handsome. They made it seem like I was soliciting an officer because I wrote my thoughts on paper. That was a bad idea! Keep in mind when you are locked up you and all your belongings, belong to the state. An officer deemed it necessary to search my stuff and started reading my journal. That's where it all began. Stay tuned for more of my story because I believe I have been called to share it. Whether through preaching or motivational speaking, I dreamed of speaking to a sea of people.

From 1994 to present I have not missed a beat. I have been gainfully employed. I have held positions I should not have. God is your guide. In order to go higher regardless of your past, you have to walk in faith. Never let others derail your journey. Surround yourself with people who inspire growth. It's okay to be alone but never stop investing in yourself—the sky's the limit.

LaToshia Simpson was born and raised in Houston, Texas where she learned early on the importance of hard work, faith, and family. She is a woman of faith, family, and purpose, and her mission is to leave a legacy that will inspire generations to come. She is a proud mother of two wonderful children and a blessed grandmother of five amazing grandchildren. After graduating high school, she pursued a career in the medical field where she earned her Medical Assistant Certification with specializations in X-ray and EKG from Remington College.

After completing my education, she began working in the healthcare industry, where she gained hands-on experience assisting patients, performing X-rays, conducting EKGs, and helping physicians provide quality care to patients. Working in healthcare gave her a deep appreciation for life, compassion, and the ability to serve others in their time of need. She transitioned to a different career path later in life, but her passion for helping others never left.

LaToshia's faith has always been the foundation of her life. She is a proud and active member of Transforming Faith Christian Center under the leadership of Pastor James and Tiffany Edwards. She firmly believes that with God, all things are possible, and that belief has carried her through many of life's challenges and victories.

LaToshia is currently employed in the public transportation industry in Austin, Texas, where she has the privilege of serving her community daily. Working in public transportation has taught her patience, compassion, and how to work with people from all walks of life..

In addition to her career, she is affiliated with Novae, a company that specializes in credit repair, financial education, business funding, and personal development. Through this platform, she offers people the tools and resources they need to improve their credit, start their own business, and build a better financial future.

Her ultimate goal is to build generational wealth, leave a lasting legacy for her family, and help as many people as possible achieve their dreams. Her journey has not always been easy, but her faith, perseverance, and commitment to success have carried me through every obstacle and opened new doors of opportunity.

I declare and decree
that God will enlarge
my territory.
I will possess and
take over the land.
I will build my business
on a solid foundation
so I can leave an
inheritance for my family.

~Deborah Franklin

NOTES

NOTES

A Journey of Healing:
Frustrated, Saved & Hurting
Michelle Boulden Hammond

I sat quietly in the back pew of the small church, my heart heavy and my faith fragile. For years, I had been deeply involved with a congregation, volunteering for nearly every ministry, counseling new members, and leading worship. Judgment, gossip, and betrayal had driven me away, leaving me spiritually wounded and emotionally broken.

It began with a critical comment from a church elder about how I led worship. People I once trusted avoided m, then I felt ostracized. My once-safe haven now felt like a battlefield and I questioned not only my place in the church but my entire faith. After months of sleepless nights and tear-filled prayers, I decided to step away.

The turning point came one evening when my friend Lesley said she had been praying for me. I realized I had been carrying my pain in silence. Through tears, I shared my story with her. I recounted the hurtful moments, the betrayal, and my confusion. She said what happened to me didn't define my faith or who I am in God's eyes, and I took the first step towards healing by acknowledging the depth of my pain and allowing someone to walk alongside me.

Encouraged by Lesley's support, I began working with a Christian therapist and I unpacked the layers of my pain. I learned that my hurt wasn't just about gossip or judgment, but the loss of trust and community I once cherished. My therapist encouraged me to journal my thoughts and prayers, which became a lifeline.

One of the hardest steps for me was forgiveness. I didn't want to forgive the people who had hurt me; I wanted them to feel the same pain I had endured. In time, I found myself releasing the bitterness that had taken root in my heart. I chose to let go of the anger by writing letters to those who had hurt me. I didn't send them, but putting my feelings on paper was cathartic.

I joined a small Bible study group at a different church, where I could observe and participate at my own pace and I began rebuilding my trust in the church. I learned to separate my faith in God from my experiences with people, understanding that while humans may fail, God's love never does.

As the healing journey progressed, I started a small support group, inviting people to share their stories and find encouragement in one another. This gave me a renewed sense of purpose, and became a platform for hope and restoration.

My journey wasn't without setbacks, but each step brought me closer to wholeness. I learned to confront my pain, seek help, forgive, and rediscover faith on my own terms. With time, support, and a willingness to heal, I transformed my pain into a purpose that not only restored me but also inspired those around her.

Dr. Michelle Boulden Hammond, PhD
Women's Wellness Practitioner | Spiritual Alignment Specialist | Sound Healing Practitioner | Singer/Songwriter | Podcast Host

Dr. Michelle Boulden Hammond is a trailblazing advocate for holistic wellness, blending her expertise in *Transpersonal Counseling* with her deep passion for empowering women to align their mind, body, and soul. As a Women's Wellness Practitioner, she helps women rediscover their inner strength, balance, and purpose through personalized, transformative experiences.

A certified Sound Healing Practitioner and gifted singer/songwriter, Dr. Hammond uses the vibrational power of music and sound to create an environment for emotional healing and spiritual growth. Her unique integration of sound therapy with spiritual alignment practices allows her clients to access deeper states of relaxation and clarity while releasing stress and tension.

Dr. Hammond is also the dynamic host of a podcast where she shares insights, interviews thought leaders, and provides tools for spiritual growth, self-care, and holistic wellness. With her magnetic voice and empathetic approach, she empowers her audience to embrace their authentic selves while navigating life's complexities.

With over a decade of experience, Dr. Hammond has become a trusted figure in the wellness community, particularly for the BIPOC community. She collaborates with community leaders and organizations, including the Maryland Health Commission, to make holistic practices accessible to all. Whether through her courses, retreats, music, or one-on-one consultations, Dr. Michelle Boulden Hammond inspires individuals to live a life of alignment, joy, and purpose.

NOTES

NOTES

The Time It Never Stopped Raining
and
I NEVER STOPPED DANCING
Dr. Sharnice Perryman

Have you ever been broken? Have you ever been fractured or damaged and no longer in one piece due to someone else's actions? Wanting to give up all hope left feeling in a state of despair? Well, let me tell you how you can be broken but beautiful.

I was minding my own business, scrolling through a dating site. Looking back, I realize I was probably trying to "help" God out. I met someone I thought could be my forever person, even though I didn't know what a narcissist was at the time. I wasn't aware of the signs or tactics of a narcissistic sociopath. Now I realize he had me the moment I initiated the conversation.

I did not know at the time however, but I had been "love bombed." He was manipulating my emotions by showering me with excessive affection right from the start. His goal from the very beginning was to gain my trust. We talked about our future together, and he pushed for an exclusive relationship. I saw it as me being swept off my feet, not realizing that those feelings would soon turn cold. He became emotionally distant and controlling.

In the beginning he seemed so impressed by my work as

a pastor and preacher. Later, I realized it wasn't about being impressed by me—it was about him being proud that he could convince someone of my stature to marry him.

This man turned out to be emotionally unavailable and he couldn't engage with me in a meaningful way. I was always longing for more, feeling misunderstood, and deeply unsatisfied emotionally. As for our sex life, him being a narcissistic sociopath he was addicted to sex. I began to feel like I was just a tool for him to satisfy his addiction.

Imagine my heartbreak when I realized he wasn't committed to the process. He didn't have the emotional capacity to love me, nurture me, or make the necessary compromises to make our marriage work.

God has a way of taking what is considered broken to show forth His beauty. But then again in my case I had to be broken, stretched and pressed in order to be further propelled into my place of purpose. He, my ex, thought he was going to break me.

Through this trial, not only was I beautifully broken, but I also learned how to suffer gracefully. This **suffering produced perseverance** and my ability to be steadfast. Ministry movements were not hindered. Being confronted with this much pain, I can always choose to fall apart and cry. And initially I did. But then, I needed to be resilient because I believe what I don't allow to kill me only makes me stronger. After each heartbreak and disappointment, I have developed the ability to bounce back, and

I always manage to move forward even through tragedy and devastation. I always come through better, stronger, more capable.

Dr. Sharnice Marie Perryman is a noted and sought-after preacher, known for her straight-forward, transparent preaching style and her unique ability to help believers to walk daily in the Word, through prophecy, deliverance and healing. Dr. Sharnice Marie Perryman is a Prophet to the Nations, and as a Firebrand she has devoted her life to God in true worship and desires to be used to motivate, inspire, and incite the Body of Christ to worship God in Spirit and in Truth. Dr. Sharnice Marie Perryman is the founder of Ladies on Purpose, which was birthed to assist individuals in discovering and walking in their God-given purpose.

After walking with the Lord for 10 years, Dr. Sharnice Marie Perryman accepted her calling and began her journey of higher learning. Dr. Perryman served in different capacities to help further the gospel at various churches. She has ministered at women's conferences and other services locally. Dr. Perryman embraces every opportunity to point people to Jesus, using her teaching, preaching, books and TV broadcasts to bring hope and direction to people across the world.

A survivor of domestic abuse, Dr. Perryman discovered how to overcome the emotional pain of her troubled past and experience to push her into her purpose. Her passion is to help others do the same by hosting her *Pain 2 Purpose* annual conference. For more than 10 years, Dr. Perryman has held conferences teaching God's Word and sharing the message of Christ with the emphasis on healing, deliverance and the prophetic. Dr. Perryman also encourages millions each day through social media and online efforts to walk in what God has called them to.

Dr. Perryman has launched two churches, Turn Around Ministries for Kingdom Living and House of Fire. Both churches focused on building the community one soul at a time. In addition to being a 4-time published author, she's also a mother of 4, grandmother, an educator as well as a Deployed Evangelist. Dr. Perryman is a proud HBCU graduate, having earned her undergraduate degree in Business Leadership from Ashford University. She also has her Honorary Doctorate Degree from Next Dimension University, and she is also the recipient of the Presidential Lifetime Achievement Award.

Dr. Perryman as a servant leader, serves from the heart, and this is why she doesn't take the credit for what God has done. If you have ever suffered any amount of loss, you'd see that Dr. Perryman is simply a woman who boldly, unapologetically and gladly loves and works for God and His people.

NOTES

_____

_____

_____

_____

_____

_____

_____

_____

_____

_____

_____

_____

_____

NOTES

I Grew Through the Grief
Chelsia McCoy

Something in my soul told me "today is the day." I knew I didn't have much time. I sat at my desk figuring out when would be the right time to grab my purse and just walk out. My manager already knew what was going on... I was okay to leave. Sure enough, my sister called and told me to come to the house. There wasn't much time left.

I took the street to my parent's house instead of the freeway. I knew I needed to get there fast, but I was dreading it at the same time. My dad was transitioning. These were the last moments of his life. He had a brain tumor that pretty much took him out quickly. He went from this vibrant man who loved listening to jazz and watching sports to a 90-pound frail person who lost his ability to walk and even speak.

I didn't know how to feel. I understood what was happening, but I wasn't ready to accept it. While sitting at a red light, I scrolled through Facebook and what I saw shook me to my core. Someone had posted "R.I.P." and my dad's name. Say what??? He was gone?? Aside from that, who knew before me – I was his daughter!

I made it to my parent's house on auto-pilot. After reading that post, I don't remember anything other than parking in the driveway and my oldest sister met me at the door. Walking down the hall to the bedroom where his hospital bed was and the hospice team was stationed was the longest walk of my life. My stomach was in my feet but I was eager and anxious to see him.

I was too late.

He had already transitioned.

I missed it.

I missed seeing his eyes open and him blinking at me to let me know he knew who I was. I missed our pinky-finger squeeze which was his way of telling me he loved me.

I cried till there were no more tears left. Now it was time to process and figure out how to heal. I wasn't new to grief. I had lost loved ones before but this was different because this was ***my daddy***. My rock. I had to pull it together because I had to be strong for my mother and my kids. Grief was put on the back burner until we got the funeral services out of the way.

We had two services – one in Texas where we lived (and his birthplace), and the other in California where my parents' burial plots had already been paid for. Leaving the cemetery, I asked myself what was next... life had to go on, but what did that look like?

Therapy was my solution. I actively and excitedly attended sessions that allowed me to vent and express my feelings while receiving tools and guidance on moving forward in the coming days. I am a huge advocate for therapy because it's truly healing for your soul. I learned how to grow *through* my pain, while adjusting to my next season of life.

For over 20 years, Chelsia McCoy has not only written her own books, but she has been helping others write their books or assist them with editing and other writing projects. Her love of writing and the written word comes from within and as she often tells people, it's in her DNA! She loved it so much she went to school and now holds a Master's degree in Communication!

In addition to working on her own books, she is the founder and CEO of *Your Writing Table*, a full-service consulting agency providing book-writing, editing, publishing, ghostwriting, and audio & video transcription services. She is also the host and producer of the popular podcast, *Women Winning at Writing*, which talks about all things writing & editing from a woman's perspective.

Her goal is to inspire and remind you that each of us has a story to tell.

Her motto: Don't wait for someone to invite you to their table... Create *your* own table and tell *your* story *your* way, in *your* words!

I declare and decree that I
will trust God in what he
shows me. I will believe the
revelation that is revealed
to me. It may make me uneasy,
but I am going forth in
Jesus' name. I will not give
up until my change comes.
I will not let go until He
blesses my soul.
~Deborah Franklin

NOTES

NOTES

Role Reversal
Dr. Deborah Franklin

Never in a million years did I ever think I would be a caregiver. I saw so many people who were, but not me. I was not expecting this but it was something I had to do. I had to accept that the roles were changing and now I had to do for my mom what she had done for me. Taking on this new role didn't come with a playbook. I had many suggestions, but no rules of engagement.

This was not supposed to be a permanent situation. We agreed you would come to live with me, get your health and finances together, then you would go back home. Who knew this would be the last time I would drive with you from your house to mine?

Our drive was full of revelations. I didn't realize you had never done this before, so really it turned into an adventure. You said, "Show me where you go when you drive back." You shocked me, I was certain you had been to these places before. . . So I took you to both places where I stopped to get goodies that I couldn't get at home.

You were so happy because you were a grocery store addict. Trust me she was in her happy place. Everything she saw she wanted to try. I felt like I was in the store with a toddler. My basket was full and I only stopped for a couple of items, but truthfully this was how it went when we would go to the grocery store or meat market. She was happy and making peace with leaving Houston where she had lived all of her adult life to make the journey to Georgia.

This was a challenging time, because soon after Mama was settled in, her health made a change. Then there was another road trip. I was shocked again. She was amazed to be riding in the hills of Tennessee. She was joining me to work on our missions project. She admitted she had never done that either. She swore up and down that she didn't come to work but to supervise. Trust me that is just what she did. One day during lunch, she was so amazed when we visited Uncle Nearest Whisky Distillery and I shared the history with her. The look of pride on her face was priceless. If I had known this would be our last road trip I would have made more stops. Mama's health got worse.

We went back and forth to the hospital and eventually had to get a hospital bed in the living room. But God knew what he was doing. My neighbors were CNA's and were able to assist me during the times I just didn't know what to do. They would come to the house, let themselves in and care for my mom.

Losing my mom was a major blow but I thank God I was able to care for her all the way to the end. Yes, I was still dealing with my grief and yes the depression came in like a storm, but I survived. I have been able to grow and expand my business. I also learned a powerful tool: I learned to ask for help.

I want to encourage you if you feel like you can't make it, just know that you can. I prayed God would send me some help and they showed up from all directions because dealing with all that goes with being a caregiver you can't do it alone.

Deborah Franklin works with high achieving women to increase their VIP (Visibility Influence Profits) by telling their stories. Deborah is the owner of DFP a full service publishing hybrid publishing company, the founder of Church Girl CEO and Church Girl CEO Foundation. Deborah has a heart for women to expand their mindsets past what they can see. As a survivor of verbal abuse, she has learned to rise above what has been said to her and about her to be the authentic representative of who she is created to be.

Deborah Franklin is the author of "Adjective," "21 Days 21 Minutes of Prayer & Meditation," and "#5 30 Days of Motivation & Inspiration," "The Prayer of Jabez In The Marketplace," podcast host of Conversations w/Deborah Franklin and a media coach. Deborah has been working as a media coach for several years with clients who are authors, speakers and entertainers.

Deborah also uses her platform to give other aspiring talents an outlet to let their talents shine. Her ultimate goal in life is to help others to ignite the power within to propel them to their destiny while walking in their destiny.

I may be transparent in telling my story, but this does not mean I'm weak or a pushover. I'm just letting them know I'm not the one to be messed with or taken for granted. I'm strong, empowered and destined for greatness.

~Deborah Franklin

NOTES

NOTES

Pray Over Them and Let Them Go
Dr. Keba Richmond Green

One of the hardest jobs in the world is being a parent. There are countless books, TV shows, and references on parenting, yet none of them fully prepare you for every situation— especially when you need guidance the most.

For many years, I was a single parent. Their fathers were in and out of their lives, but my children had a loving and dependable village that stepped in to support us. After years of struggling, failed relationships, and countless sacrifices, I was finally blessed to remarry the one I knew was meant for me.

However, becoming a wife did not erase my single-mother mentality overnight. It took time, patience, and growth. I was so used to doing everything on my own that whenever my husband tried to step in to discipline or guide my children I would instinctively become defensive. My fierce protection over my children's emotions often led me to push him away, even though he was the partner I had prayed for. After years of internal battles, I finally learned to yield and submit, allowing him to take his rightful place as the head of our home, and we finally found our balance.

As my children grew into young adults, they started

allowing the world to influence their decisions, and our bond faced its greatest test. They graduated high school, began asserting their independence, and soon became completely out of control.

I spent countless nights pacing the floor in prayer, crying out for them, pleading with God to cover them. My spirit was restless. Then one night, I distinctly heard the Lord say, "Pray over your kids and let them go."

I hesitated and the voice came again, unwavering: "Pray over them and let them go."

I cried even harder. I wrestled with the idea for months. Eventually, I found the strength to obey. I gathered my children, prayed over them, and released them into God's hands. Then I asked them to leave our home, trusting that God would take care of the rest.

Months later, I received the worst phone call of my life. My daughter had been shot. I was six hours away when I heard the news, and I immediately turned to prayer. As she fought for her life, losing and regaining consciousness three times on the operating table, I held on to my faith. By God's grace, she survived. Through that painful experience, God showed me something powerful—He is in control, not me.

Why does it often take tragedy, sickness, or loss for us to lean fully into Him? We say we trust Him, yet we try to hold on to what He's asking us to release. This lesson taught me that no matter what, God is my source and my strength. Our children are only loaned to us for a time—to guide, direct, and correct. And when the time comes, we must give them back to Him, trusting that He will cover them in ways we never could.

In all things, trust God. Trust the process. And then, trust God again.

Dr Keba Richmond-Green, PhD., LPC: Licensed Marriage & Family Psychoanalyst, Relationship Coach, Consultant, Published Author, International Speaker, and Visionary.

Keba Richmond Green is an entrepreneur who owns and operates many businesses. She works from a family system's approach and believes in theory that an individual cannot exist and cannot be understood except in their relation to the whole family. She works to help individuals find their place and purpose in the system, work inwards so the outer shines. The only way to affect change is the willingness to change yourself.

I will be a positive leader of my tribe. I will empower them to reach their fullest potential and encourage them to reach for the stars. I will continue to learn new things to share with my tribe and keep the excitement growing for my members.

~Deborah Franklin

NOTES

_____

_____

_____

_____

_____

_____

_____

_____

_____

_____

_____

_____

NOTES

_____

_____

_____

_____

_____

_____

_____

_____

_____

_____

_____

_____

The Other Side of Life After Divorce: The First Lady

Syreeta Duncan

In October of 2010 I became the wife of a minister and later gained the title as a "First Lady." I have always had a Baptist upbringing, so I was no newbie to the "church" life, circles, and cliches. But what I was new to was being at the forefront as a first lady. I knew absolutely nothing about being anything other than me. I was rocking a short, colored hair style, with a bubbly, friendly, snobbish, shy, don't talk to me at all, kind of attitude.

He thought the world of his first family and his home church LOVED him, so I wanted to be a pleasing representation. I took fast to the First Lady position, eager to learn and become the woman the "church" wanted me to be. Now, I knew my husband, the Baptist pastor, would be very judgmental of me because he had married someone like me. I was eight years older than him with two kids, so I wasn't the ideal first lady in their eyes. But as God gave His assignments for the 10-year duration of my marriage and my "First Lady" era, I learned so many life lessons as a First Lady: speak less and watch more, don't chew gum, always smile, always have a lap cloth, people don't like you in church business, talk to everyone after church, everyone wants to be friends with the first lady, and they judge the first lady harder than they judge the pastor.

Life after being a divorced First Lady was eye opening. I was emotionally, mentally and physically depressed. I had mastered how to smile through everything. It took so much of me; the title itself was a job and "church" began feeling like a job, too. I was no longer free to express my praise openly, I was unhappy in a marriage where I wasn't heard or understood or supported outside of the church, covered lies and broken promises, drained from trying to make it work; and later feeling like God had forsaken me after divorce. I tried to understand and find peace, while staying focused on God.

I was lost, so confused, feeling betrayed by God and disgusted that I had gone through a divorce from the man of God. It took four years for me to enter church as Syreeta again. No longer holding on to those imperfections of me, each day gets better. If I could leave the title holders of *First Lady* and the divorcees anything, I would say, always be true to you, trust God even when things aren't great, and marry a partner that listens and chooses every version of you daily.

Syreeta Duncan is a resident of Montgomery, Alabama. She has been recognized by many organizations for her leadership both in community and as a female entrepreneur.

Currently, Ms. Duncan is the second African American female to own a professional basketball organization in Alabama. It is her goal to use professional basketball to help the youth and her community. She believes it's more than the game of basketball, but it is a sport that helps build character, leadership, discipline, determination, and teamwork.

Syreeta is an author, business owner, life and relationship coach, a motivational speaker, and a breast cancer survivor activist. She is a firm believer, that with God nothing is impossible but all things are possible.

AFFIRMATIONS

Affirmations are good for the soul. We have to wake up winning in our minds, hearts and souls. We have to show up ready to fly high and accomplish our goals. We are destined to live the VIP Luxury lifestyle we desire and deserve. We have to confess with our mouth and believe in our heart that it will come to pass now!

Use these affirmation to amplify your voice to yourself and to the world. It's your time to be heard.

I AM.........................

- ➢ **Beautiful!**
- ➢ **Fearless!**
- ➢ **Powerful!**
- ➢ **Unstoppable!**
- ➢ **Resilient!**
- ➢ **Unapologetically me!**
- ➢ **Able to move in the marketplace as a leader!**
- ➢ **Not going to let anything that someone says get me down!**

I declare and decree that I will oversee and operate my business, my family and my life to glory and honor God. I will not flinch in the eyes of my adversaries or let doubt flood my mind. I will be influential in my area of expertise.

~Deborah Franklin

I am a Queen! I am a Queen!

With style and grace, I will rule my

business and family with fairness,

empathy and productivity.

I can do this, and I will do this!

In Jesus name, Amen.

~Deborah Franklin

I was born to lead;

therefore, I will lead.

I am empowered and I will

empower others to reach

their fullest potential.

~Deborah Franklin

I declare and decree this is my visibility season. I will be seen and heard. I will no longer operate in the shadows of my own self-doubt. I will shine bright in every room I occupy.

~Deborah Franklin

My heart and mind are open to the people and resources that God is sending my way! They may not look like me or act like me, but they are who I need in this season to bring my vision to life.

~Deborah Franklin

I declare and decree that this is my

Grand Opening. I'm cutting the

ribbon on my new attitude,

my new business ventures,

my new relationships and my

expectations of what God

is sending my way!

~Deborah Franklin

I will live my life in a state of happiness. I will embrace the circumstances that I'm in and won't let them get me down. I know that God is with me and my faith is strong.

~Deborah Franklin

I am a vaulted diamond. I am not for everyone and will not be treated like a cubic zirconia. I will not crack under pressure or break when pushed in a corner.
I know my worth!
I have clarity and
I am not for everyone!

~Deborah Franklin

I will be strong and mighty as I take over the land that God has called me to! My life is blessed and prosperous. I will conquer every circumstance that arises. My nay-sayers will be under my feet and cast out of my mind back to the pits of hell from whence it came!

~Deborah Franklin

God is the author of my day and my life. I write stories of success, prosperity, abundance and each page of my life helps me to become a better version of myself.

~Chelsia McCoy

NOTES

NOTES

NOTES

NOTES

_____

_____

_____

_____

_____

_____

_____

_____

_____

_____

_____

_____

NOTES

NOTES

NOTES

At Deborah Franklin Publishing (DFP), we pride ourselves on being a full-service publishing house that is large enough to serve you, yet small enough to need you. We believe in providing personalized attention to all our clients, recognizing that each author and their book have unique goals and aspirations.

From the very beginning, we are here to assist you every step of the way, from the inception of your book idea to the final stages of publishing and launching. Our dedicated team of award-winning editors and designers will work closely with you, ensuring that your vision is brought to life and that your manuscript reaches its full potential.

Our editors are not only experienced but have also been recognized for their excellence in the industry. They will meticulously review your manuscript, providing insightful feedback, and ensuring that your writing is refined and polished. Our designers, on the other hand, will collaborate with you to create captivating cover designs and interior layouts that will catch the eye of your target audience.

At DFP, we understand that publishing a book is just the first step. That's why we go beyond traditional publishing services. We act as your personal concierge for all your publishing and marketing needs. Whether it's strategizing your book launch, implementing effective marketing campaigns, or exploring distribution options, we are here to guide and support you throughout the entire process.

Your success is our priority, and we are dedicated to being by your side as you embark on your publishing journey. With our expertise and commitment, we strive to be the catalyst for your accomplishments as an author.

We look forward to working with you and helping you achieve your publishing goals.

www.ingramcontent.com/pod-product-compliance
Lightning Source LLC
Chambersburg PA
CBHW051538120626
46551CB00013B/1272